Pepin Diary

dougie padilla

LUNA BRAVA PRESS
Pepin, Wisconsin

First Printing: 2019

ISBN 978-1-7330911-0-7

LUNA BRAVA PRESS
202 Main Street
Box 146
Pepin, WI 54759

www.dougiepadilla.com

Cover photo: Dougie Padilla

Cover design: Pete Sandvik, Perfect Circle Creative

Publications manager: Karen Wilcox

LUNA BRAVA PRESS
Pepin, Wisconsin

this is for the grands:

Douglas José
Carlos Gabino
Paloma Isabel
Liliana Alicia
Amaya Angélica
Felicity Modesto
Jefferson Alejandro

god bless.

"If the Angel decides to come
it will be because you have convinced her,
not by tears, but by your humble resolve
to be always beginning; to be a beginner."

- Rainer Maria Rilke

contents

contents

last night

last night,
coming home from a friend's
little cabin in the woods,
moon bigger than full,
low and wide over the road to pepin,
no other cars in sight,

i felt the full sirens' call,
i heard the enchantress's subtle song,
deer in the weeds off the shoulder,
just waiting to dive in front of my truck
and give their souls to god and gods
and whatever fairies surrounded us.

next full moon on the solstice
is in 2094 they say.
i'll be 146 then - well, 145.
i won't turn 146 til well over a month later.

i dream about it now.
the softness is compelling.
i have grown larger than the lake i live beside:

once again, there are moths in my ears,
dancing away in the light.
once again, there are songs unraveling,
right there at the beginning of the dream.

solstice seems to be the exact height of silence.
it seems to have wandered off to norway
and the quiet home on sognefjord
where we all spent our early days.

i am a poet now. i am a poetess.
one of my eyes moves to the side of my head, like a fish.
turkey vultures sit on the jetty nearby,
staring at me, maybe 10 of them.
the breeze is clean and new,
and wanders in from over past lake city.

i have not come this far to stop now.
pain will not hold me back.
i refuse to disappear into the internet,
into wine and beer, into sex.
i refuse to take lightly my proximity
to the passing world,
to the next world,
to the world we are waiting for.

the lilacs have bloomed and fallen back asleep.
my hammock sits empty in the yard.
for once, i will turn my chair around
and face the street,
wave to all that pass by,
and mumble,
delicately to myself,
about angels and dragonflies
and the short sweet smell of sunset.

dog lust joy

it is spring.
the air grows delicious
each morning as I peak my head
out the door
for the morning paper
on the steps.

and each morning
the dog wakes
from her station on the couch,
heads for the sliding door
in susan's office
where she oversees
the scene out the back door.
susan feeds the birds,
mostly sparrows,
but, also, the occasional blue jay
or cardinal.

they knock half their seed
off the feeders
to the deck
where squirrels and chipmunks
grow fat
off our largesse.

staring thru
the pane of glass,
stella squeals with anticipation,
her blood surging,
150 years of breeding
pounding to the forefront

of her coonhound mind.
I roll the door open
and she digs her claws
into the deck wood
sprinting with every fiber in her
hound body,
howling in delight
as she turns the corner,
sprints down the stairs
and punishes every bit of the yard
with her dog lust joy.

monday night football

watching the vikes
get shellacked by chicago,
favre knocked out in the 2nd period,
probably his last game –
he had a good long run.

at the same time
reading some of the beats,
corso, lew welch, whalen, snyder,
even a little kerouac,
mostly during the commercials.

welch, especially, is a revelation.
god i loved him in the sixties.
he's no less wonderful now,
tho i myself am in my sixties.

"Sausalito Trash Prayer"
"Song of the Turkey Buzzard"
"[The Image as in a Hexagram]"
"[The Empress Herself Served Tea
 to Su Tung-po,]" -
all big faves, all still delightful.

but it is "[I Saw Myself]"
that is the masterpiece.
and "ring of bone" –
how many of us will have
that exact golden moment?
how many of us will continue
to long for that one small auspicious event
that stretches out

throughout the rest of our lives
and into eternity?

its the 4th quarter now.
favre is still out,
the rookie joe webb is in the game.
we look kinda hopeless –
even the defense seems lost.
when the bears win,
it guarantees them the division title -
and makes the packers' dilemma
that much harder, thank god.

tomorrow i will wake up around 6,
eat, check my email, meditate.
then i'll go out into the cold winter wind
and shovel snow
under the deep, bright blue sky.

and i will be quite happy.

may all beings know peace.
may all beings find awakening.

ben

last night suzie castro
came all the way from colombia
in my dreams.
she sat behind me
and massaged my aching neck.

i woke up happy
and sent my love to her this morning,
blessed her and the boys
and the spirit of her long gone husband ben,
my friend,
my son's close friend,
dead of cancer of the brain so young.

we all cried at that funeral –

all of us.

there were angels everywhere.
they seemed to flock towards our sorrow,
towards the beauty of our grief,
moths to a flame.
they must have had some strange desire
to annihilate
what little there is of themselves
in the longing,
in the light.

++++

i close the front door of the studio,
its too cold for fresh air.
i'll meditate and walk the dog soon.

maren wants to do tai chi up in stockholm.
maybe i'll make a pork chop for lunch
and work on that big painting
i started long ago.

or maybe i'll just lie down on the couch for a bit,
pet my dog,
and fall asleep
as i listen to the leaves

drop from the trees

outside my door.

its dark out yet.

its dark out yet.
6a.m
winter in minnesota.
the dog's asleep on the couch upstairs.
susan is asleep in her bedroom,
the cat curled next to her head.
the city is still asleep,
or just waking up.
an occasional bus
bounces by on the streets.

hell, lots of folks in this country
are still asleep.
but the blubbery bear in his golden den
is just waking up.
he brushes his teeth
with his solid gold toothbrush
wearing golden pajamas
then he turns on the cable tv networks
on his huge gold tv.
immediately he is outraged
(his is the best outrage)
and starts looking for his gold phone.
his first tweet of the morning will be gold,
he's sure of that.
he's looking forward to breakfast,
he only has the best breakfasts
(on gold gilded plates
with solid gold forks and spoons).
sitting at the golden dining room table,
he doesn't bother with the lying media
and their lying newspapers.

he's looking forward to the bowl of candy,
(tart yet sweet hard candy
in solid gold wrappers),
sitting on his immense desk,
the best desk in the world,
where he will make all the right decisions today,
and the world will love him even more,
love him, the best,
the very best leader in the world.

++++++

i've been in the city four days now.
i've started to miss the country.
the vultures have been gone from pepin
for four months.
i miss their constant circling presence,
high up drifting in the thermals,
the softness of their
constant search from the air,
the knowledge that death
never seems to escape them.

i wonder if the huge bear
will die in office.
if he will get up in the middle
of the night to pee,
as all old bulbous men do,
a trickling, sprinkling
tidbit of pee
finding its way
to the bowl beneath him;
if he will sit on the toilet,
lost in the moment,
the dark moment,

the darkest moment,
and then slump to the floor,
his term of office,
the best presidency ever,
ended, ended in the way it began,
unconscious, a soap opera moment,
in a soap opera life,
the best soap opera life.

poem for the guru

i keep remembering how the green parrot
landed on your mike stand
while you described the path to heaven.

you were always so blissed out...
i swear there was nobody home.
i loved all the singing and dancing.
and the melody of your voice.

i was missing my children,
2 and 4 and back in the states.
i missed them desperately.
so god gave me hepatitis
the day after my 30th birthday party,
and i lay on the roof of our flat
in the untouchable village across the river
from the ashram,
lost from my body
for 56 straight days.

then one morning,
as i watched the rickshaws race by,
as i watched the women smash their laundry
against the river rocks,
it all melted into oneness,
into the great life river,
and there was no me,
and no you,
no problems,
no sadness...
not even joy.

today i sit in an outdoors café,
part of the holiday inn complex,
here south of winona,
where i spent so much of my youth.

i'm having the greek gyros sandwich plate
with sweet potato fries.
there's a soft cool breeze,
its pleasant here,
so i delay awhile.
but soon, i'll head for rochester.
judy's gonna fill my truck with junk,
good junk,
art junk.

we'll probably have dinner,
maybe with burt, her husband.
it's always special to visit them.

then, i'll head back upriver
in my big black pickup,
follow the mississippi,
underneath the massive full moon
until i make it to my studio in pepin,
and my wonderful soft bed.

who knows why we live the lives we live?
who knows why we are being given
this immense gift?

each moment gorgeous beyond understanding.

gulls

gulls everywhere in the skies this dusk.
they're gorging on mayflies.

the guy on the air mattress floats by again.

i think I'll relearn how to sing.

68

grandchildren about.
carlos on the couch
immersed in a pokemon book,
paloma in her party dress
helping my daughter
make me my birthday breakfast.
waffles i think.

sixty-eight years old today:
robins' eggs the size of basketballs
fall from the sky,
not one breaks.
fat trees everywhere begin to sing
(mostly in farsi, but some in what appears
to be a sub-dialect of hindi).
and the refrigerator wants to talk,
walk and talk.
again.

despite the pain in my back,
i am happy.

well, happy except for the groaning
slow strain of ice on the lake back home,
blue, translucent, lonely, alive.
how can i miss winter?
what kinda fool wants to go back to five below?

its hot here, i guess.
really hot, too hot.
la mesa, city of hills, so-cal kinda hot.
plus, there's way too much concrete in this town.

hot, dusty concrete,
car concrete,
truck concrete,
mall concrete.

today i am getting myself a massage,
a respite from the world of gravity.
later, i will meditate like the seraphim,
(sexless, heavenly, deeply silent, almost sullen)
and visit the in-laws' taqueria
on washington street,
much nearer downtown.

for this birthday,
i wanna fly again,
this time not just in my dreams.
i want to fly to the next world and back.
while i'm there i want to see my father,
all my dogs,
my guru,
and w.c. wormley,
king of nordeast artists.

god, i hope billy's happy now,
that he's still painting.
and i hope ruby's there
at his feet,
faithful to the last,
the best dog
ever.

abby

1.

abby the chihuahua mix,
mellow as her white bearded
hipster so-cal owner.
seniors banging away
on the paddle board courts:

pong...
pong...
pong...

few parks here in la mesa,
gotta dig hard for them,
tho gps might work.
cool ocean breeze
wanders in from the ocean.
homeless guy sleeps on the lawn.

across the way,
a retiree combs the grass
with his metal detector,
most likely hoping to find
the lost gold of cortez.

2.

back hurt all night
time to do tai chi,
squirm around in this package of flesh
until some kind of truce is reached.

i wonder if i can be reborn
as a madrone tree,
so gorgeous,
stately,
pain-free.

maybe if i put my order in now.
i know i'm supposed to stay in the human form,
circle of life,
wheel of reincarnation and all that.
no harm in trying tho.

3.

how many different greens are there?
i mean look out your eyes this mid-summer
and just see the greens,
greens like an artist sees greens.
its endless.

the buddha didn't worry about greens.
i'm pretty sure obama doesn't
(unless we count ecology here).
chagall focused more on blue,
as did klein.

but right now i sit at a green picnic table
in a sea of green just off palm avenue,
la mesa, California,
and i wonder
why the madrones have decided
to run up this hillside,
why the skies are so desperately blue,

and why we have created a world

filled

with an ocean of gnats.

for james mejia

the snow came in long hard waves all night
til this morning i woke
with a good solid foot of pretty wet stuff
hugging the ground.

it was the snowplow that woke me,
driving madly
up and down second street, then main,
a blaze orange dump truck bull
charging madly
at unseen red flags.

i talked to eric over at paul and fran's,
he's been here his whole life,
and he can't discern any pattern
to the plowing either.
i think the county drivers
are using this village as their canvas,
modernists throwing paint
whichever way the moment allows.
kinda hard to figure out where to park tho.

no matter.

i gotta move this stuff off the sidewalk as best i can.
wondering at 68 how much longer i should do this,
maybe i should start farming it out.
but damn i do love shoveling snow.
nothing better than working up a good sweat
on a gorgeous white winter day,
using my sweet body like an athlete again,
tossing shovel load after shovel load
out into the street.

suddenly, i think of james mejia.
six foot two, pole skinny, hard muscled,

black puerto rican from the city,
all afro'd out, a dark halo surrounding
his grinning, stoned eyes,
running down the mile long
driveway from the commune
to where we stood,
shovels in hands
trying to dig out of the mud
the school bus
we'd turned into a pick-up truck
with torches.

it took six of us
and two tractors to pull
that baby free.
by the time it was flying home
to the commune
we were all covered with mud
to our knees.
and james,
james was happy,
a happy man.

cause james mejia always ran to trouble.

cause trouble was where the action was,
trouble was where the moment was most alive,
trouble was so much more interesting

than the vacant sloth
of easy.

spring of '74,
trempealeau county,
wisconsin

plum city

vikings won last night.
4-0 now.
best start in a long time.

defense continues to shine.
offense stumbles,
but is almost adequate.
hard getting my hopes up tho,
been a fan too long.

watched the game at the bear's den,
typical wisconsin country bar.
talked to my neighbors next to me,
they were from minnesota too,
here to get away,
spending the odd day at the trailer park
across the highway.

the sun comes out.
i eat a bit of chocolate
and dream of mexico.
i miss my cousin ventura,
my uncle alfredo.
they're gone now,
i'll have to find them on the other side.
i'm told that won't be hard,
that they'll be there waiting for me
when i arrive.
we'll see.

sugar maple beginning to turn,
the yellows and oranges alive

and winding their way down through the leaves.
a week and the bluffs will be lit up.
two weeks and they'll be all on fire.
the deer will be anxious in the woods,
the bear will start moving less and less.
my neighbor will drink less
so his trigger hand is steadier.
he needs fresh meat for the winter.

soon i'll step inside
and begin the process of making art,
a fool's game if ever there were one.
sometimes the water changes into wine,
sometimes it changes back again.
if i'm lucky today,
i'll hear the odd riff of coltrane in the air,
or catch a bit of chagall in the way i see.

and then, maybe,
if the light is just right,
there will be an angel in my pen
as i scratch on paper for hours,
drifting over and over again,
up against the stars in the night sky,
just outside plum city.

ugly heads

i keep wanting my poems
to burst into surrealist flame,
ducks melting into golden fire hydrants.

but instead,
zen-like haiku
rear their ugly heads,
and the very nature of reality
is released
from the rows of identical condos
where it dwells,
alone,

lost in the suburbs.

the cold took most of what we had.

the cold took most of what we had.

it was the bitter stuff,
the cold where your nostrils freeze shut,
where it burns your lungs to take a breath,
the cold that sits in your bones
and complains miserably
until you find a sauna,
a hot tub,
a bath.

tomorrow morning
i'm sure the sparrows will freeze in the trees,
fall on the sidewalks,
shatter like glass,
shards scattering into the deep snow.

i'm tired of living in this time,
in this place.
there is a stink to the world,
some kind of rot.
how can things rot
when it's this cold?

++++++++

trump turns his head
slowly to the right
and we all watch
the lights in the room
begin to fade.

actually, there is no light
available at all,
only dimness,
only scratching noise,
the noise a radio makes
in southwestern minnesota,
the dial lost between stations,
out on gravel roads,
far from any sign of life,
far from human beings.

++++++++

i'm young,
this is not a time for forgiveness,
there will be time for that later.

no, this is the time
to have bones in our feet,
in our knees.
time for small silver fish
to swim up our spines
to our heads,
into our waking brains,
while we stammer on about the old days
and the ones that walked
all the way back from Verdun,

solo,

alone,

dragging their rifles
in the mud.

it was more of the sleep game

last night it was more of the sleep game,
the body too hot for covers,
the mind roaming over each and every soul
that came to celeste's salon at the 404:
i could see so much,
the vision went so far in,
so many souls, so much information.
but, the voice was calming.
the voice was home...

around five i drifted
into some space between sleep and waking,
and, then, once again,
the backyard was completely crowded
with yacking birds.

 once again, they were quizzing me:

"what is the sound of one hand clapping?",
"what is the buddha nature of a dog?",
"what was your face before your mother was
born?"

they think they're wise,
i think they're arrogant.

++++

ok, now the birds are singing beautifully.
no more smart aleck koan study,
no more zen master ruse.

they've hit the mark,
time has slowed down...
each note a small symphony,
each song a poem.

the sun has risen,
there are no clouds in the sky.
the grass is green,
the lake is blue.

we are all hard wired
for this mission,
like it or not.

laptop

1.

i sit at my laptop,
the news is just too much.
should i silence my life,
stop reading papers,
stop looking at facebook,
stop listening to my radio?

i think i could grow quieter that way,
i could let my stomach settle,
i could watch my mind grow numb.
of course, then i would be just another guy

sipping on a beer
as the blackshirts
march across italy,

just another guy
munching on cheesy breads
as the brownshirts
descend on unionists
in munich.

2.

it is mid-winter,
everywhere i look is either white or gray.
the days are short,
the light is dying by four.
i spend my time shuffling around the studio

in this small village,
half-lost from life,
next to a great lake,
half-dead from pollution.

when i get up the energy i'll meditate.
maybe the gods will dance with my soul today,
maybe the light will sprint
up throught the nadis
through the crown chakra
and light up
all the accompanying delights.
its happened before.
i've learned to not demand it.

later, i'll eat lunch and walk the dog downriver,
out along the chippewa.
she'll spend an hour living thru her nose,
i'll spend an hour
sharpening my mind
into ice and wind.

3.

in the dream there are no sharp angles,
there is no sludge at the bottom of the pool.
in the dream we all float like eagles,
circling, circling, circling...

4.

i want to walk into the trees forever.

i want the deer to learn my tongue.
i want my grandchildren to live
in the field next door
so that i can find them easily.

i want the fish to stop swimming upstream,
to turn around,
drift past me where i stand,
and blossom into pale pink rose petals,
falling on us all
the way the milky way
fell on my sinking heart,
lost in david's boat mid-river,
lost in the darkness,
lost in that august night

not so long ago.

too much jabber

1.

too much jabber,
tv's on as a i move
from room to room.
car noise from the freeways,
planes overhead.
mechanical noise.
brain jabber.

cicada goes off,
that high, high pitched whine,
the lightest touch of cool breeze
where i 've moved to on the deck,
under the pergola,
backyard,
northeast minneapolis.

2.

68 years now.
how'd that happen?
time speeds up, slows down,
disappears down a rabbit hole
as i walk the dog
along the river.

3.

my dog stella's a coonhound,
such a strange blend of absolute innocence
and trail smart dog world aggression.
one moment fast asleep
in my lap on the couch,
(no small beast),
the next racing out the door,
her growl blaring at intruders
thru the seven-foot chain link fence,
their owners leading them
lazily to the park nearby.

4.

will i melt today?
will the heat consume this body?
will the humidity suffocate
whatever it is i am
in this blind hole
of turpitude?

5.

a hanging curve ball comes my way.
i've been waiting for this moment my entire life.
low and outside,
but still within the strike zone.
i can reach it,
knock it down the right field line.
i just have to hold back a bit,
not be too eager,
not be too eager.

6.

once i found katagiri roshi,
all black robes and shaved head,
playing with my two-year old son
in his buddhist book lined study
in the apartment above the zendo.
he had a three-foot step ladder
to reach all his books.
it was all squeals and giggles
as they took turns
parachuting off the top rung
to the carpet floor
far, far below.

bill's place

(for w.c. wormley)

art and junk piled high,
only narrow paths to navigate,
a black, dirty dog by our feet.

sitting in the cold,

bullshitting by the space heater.

seven a.m.

the light is brand new.
linda travels up and down 2nd street
on her riding lawnmower.
she is the elder goddess
of hanging petunia plants
and waters them accordingly.

a morning dove sings along with the air
conditioners.

the mayflies have arrived.
they come in waves,
crashing into my studio building
like the mongol hordes
driving west thru poland.
design-wise, kind of a gaudy bug,
all wings and long looping tail.
i'll dodge them the best i can.

a morning dove sings along with the air
conditioners.

stella is over in the weeds
that used to be my neighbors back yard.
there is something very interesting there.
if she finds just exactly the right rabbit,
perhaps she will run and run
and then take wing and join the constellations
i sat and watched like t.v.
last night out on the breakwater.
she'd be the constellation "stella".
or maybe she'll just sit with her nose in the air
creating worlds across the galaxy

in her dog mind.

a morning dove sings along with the air
conditioners.

we live in a strange world.
we cram ourselves up against each other in cities
until we're crazy - then we act crazy
and shoot god knows how many folks
at country music festivals.
once when i was around 12,
i caught a dozen or so gophers
out on the golf course
and put them in a cage i'd made.
i wanted to be some kinda scientist
and see how they lived, how they interacted.
they ate each other in a few days.

a morning dove sings along with the air
conditioners.

linda goes about her duties.
she is winding her way thru the stars
up 35 towards the solar system
known as the village of stockholm.
her wings hang loosely from her shoulders,
her perpetual cigarette dangles from her lips.
every petunia in this county is in love with her,
every golf cart this side of the big river
wants to have her moon child.
we all pay homage to her ways.

a morning dove sings along with the air
conditioners.

trump is in the news once more.

trump is in the news once more.
i read on my iphone that he doesn't trust
most of his aides.

i think his hearing is failing him,
the connection between his ears and his mind
shorted out.
maybe it has something to do
with that hair of his,
maybe the orange dye he uses on it
has seeped thru his scalp
thru his cranium,
thru his brain
and into the sheets on the bed
where he doesn't sleep with melania,
melania lost in that huge gilded apartment
in new york city,
the president lost in the capital,
unable to find the toilet
in the middle of the night.

at 3 a.m. he can't sleep either,
but his body is not filled with marbles,
his body is filled with nails and tacks
and sharp objects made in foreign countries
that we owe lots of money.

there is no position he finds comfortable now.
each move he makes lasts for only a minute
and then he must move again.

he's wondering if there's a way

he can get out of this,
if going back home is possible.

but what would "back home" be
for a man who eats his subordinates daily,
for a man who tears apart
and gorges on those
that do not bring him his due?

mayflies

1.

mayflies cover my face and arms
as i walk the dog
above lake pepin,
the outlook
just before maiden rock.
they have transparent wings
and long curling tails.

out across the river,
a barge crosses
in front of inspiration point.

2.

driving down river,
immature eagles
circle and soar overhead
as i push
my not even remotely politically correct
pickup truck
on to the village of pepin.

last night at the party
i was in people's minds again.
when i touched their bodies
i could see and feel their pain,

i could touch their sickness.

3.

texting all morning about the cops
and "black lives matter"
and all the ramifications of empire.
sweating through my shirt.

i miss my wife already.

i've been gone three hours.

4.

when the soul flies between worlds
a kind of singing happens.
i long for that exact sound.

bright white full moon

1.

bright white full moon
rising to my left,
downriver,
must be over wabasha.

bright orange sun
sinking into the trees,
upriver,
kinda over stockholm.

thousands of mayflies
hovering in the evening sky
all antennae and tails and wings and eyes.
(did you know that they don't eat,
just hatch eggs and die in a few days?)

someone floats by
on an air mattress
on their back,
gulls lilting across the jetty,
bluffs turning hazy as the light dies.

ate well tonight,
a couple of spicy sausages,
brussel sprouts sautéed in butter,
toasted organic raisin nut bread,
apple pie,
a spotted cow beer.

2.

there is only one world,
no matter what they say.

3.

the river turns a gentle blue and silver
and i ruminate about leaving that one world.
mayflies want to lay eggs in my ears,
but i ask them to back off.
gulls sing stevie wonders'
"songs in the key of life",
the whole album, from the beginning,
all the way through.
i ask the streets to remain solid
and not disappear
when i am not paying attention.

3.

i am lonely.
i am not lonely.

someday soon i will be gone.
i will live forever.

the badger digs his hole
up in the bluffs.
donald trump babbles on,
unaware of his surroundings.
trains run up the far shore
from winona to red wing.

i make art,
even in my sleep.

i make art,
even in my sleep.

awake. asleep.

woke up this morning
body & soul
all shattered.
spent half the night trying to cleanse.
too many vibes to handle.

awake.
asleep.

mow lawn.
visit dr. yu and his needles.
stop by and water the plants
at stan & ardy's graves.
drop off art as a wedding present
for scott and kate.

the sun lengthens out as the morning passes.
where does it come from?
where does it go?
who is asking?

had an argument at the party last night.
i cannot drink beer
(i had two).
i cannot handle being around drinking.
i cannot handle the way
other people's thoughts
enter my body.

there's a stillness now.
not one single cloud in the sky.
no sign of angels either.

should write notes to tina/luis/davie.
i couldn't make their events.
cause i've gotten bat-shit psychic.
is that a good thing?

help josh move a table later with the truck.
did i say mow the lawn?
pack for pepin.

a long spider web reaches
delicately
all the way
from the hanging plant
to the table.
how optimistic.

i need to go back undercover.
i need to stop snoring out loud.
i need the grandchildren
to become my eyes and ears.
i would like the grass to stop growing,
but still stay green.

early march

chopped
ice
chunks
groaning
in the river.
maybe 40 eagles
sit
at the water's frozen edge
a mile out
or so.

stella,
joyous
at being off-leash,
dances
across the jetty,
suddenly
looking back
to make sure
i still exist.

then,
startled
by critter smells,
she forgets me
completely
and tiptoes
her way
across the rocks

thru
nose
heaven.

backyard august morning

backyard august morning,
breeze keeping the bugs down.
bj sick and recovering in maiden rock.
wondering how to pass on word
to common friends.

another strange night's sleep,
been a strange year that way.
wake often to pee,
heart rumbling.
more half-assed rest,
too many days in a row.

the a.c. kicks on again,
even tho it's cool out.
spiders super busy,
cobwebs everywhere.
enterprising little fucks.

today i won't work on art
for cassady's dada show,
art which, by law, i absolutely
cannot take seriously.
best to put all that off.

neither will i write about my wife today.
how can i miss her so -
its been just a day!

god that's pathetic.

so much for learning to be alone.

for rufino tamayo

sitting in the backyard at the studio,
typing on my laptop,
which is sitting on top
of a book on rufino tamayo,
the great mexican painter
(who looks like my grandpa).
the text is by octavio paz
and some french guy i've never heard of
(i usually just look at the pictures,
but its octavio paz and maybe
i gotta give the essay a try).

a beige ford f150 drives by,
two sailboards perched in back,
one with a red bottom,
the other half yellow,
both headed toward the big lake
for a bright, beautiful summer day,
songbirds chirping away
all around me.

suddenly its all drowned out
by the guy from "third base bar"
as he mows the grass next door,
his big honkin' john deere sit-down mower
pounding this morning's brilliant life
into cubes of broken auto parts
and pools of stagnant used garage oil.

this world was not built for machines.
this world is woven daily
from slight strands of light

and the lightest of flowering fragrances
as they fall across my face
in bed in the morning.
the stillness of turtles waking
is in that soup.
cicadas just learning to sing
are in that soup.

and so is my dog
sleeping in the sun
over by seifert's place,

hot and happy,

and submerged in a sea of love.

perfect

a hour and three birthday waffles later
i chase the grandkids,
"monster bappo",
growling,
all grumpy faces
and plodding feet.
squeals and laughter abound.

i rarely catch them.

i am perfectly

inadequate.

chicken waffle world

i'm tired.

this aging thing is not all its cracked up to be.
time gets all weird when your sleep is weird.
did i say i'm tired?

been reading ginsberg on the toilet,
"america".
he put his queer shoulder to the wheel.
i don't have a queer shoulder,
but i was painting in my dreams again,
the whole next painting:
glowing light surrounding the body,
colors flowing from the chakras,
energy splurting thru the top of my being
out into the heavens.
who knows what it will look like
when it's done.
the body is a silly thing.

i think about the chicken waffle doughnut
over at "glam doughnuts".
and about putin and his little weasel brain.
and how dangerous it is to be a weasel brain,
a weasel brain
in a chicken waffle world.

plus, it was foggy this morning here in the city.
in my poems the dog is always sleeping
next to me on the couch.
i wear red paint splattered crocks

to keep my hopes alive.
i'm thinking of entering a celebrity
mystic reality show,
something where i can
put my interests to good use.

then there's trump.
the crazies have taken the war to pepin,
a "go back to mexico" sign
on the steps of the coffee shop,
the owner, spanish-american from kenosha.
he does look kinda dark tho,
in a heavy metal way.
you'd think that racists would
get their facts straight,
me the only mexican in the village,
in the township too,
this white norwegian body
housing some mexican dna,
nobody smart enough to threaten dougie,
the real source of decay in the neighborhood.

i can hear the birds now.
spring has come two months early,
(no global warming here!).
cars fly down 2nd street,
into the sides of buildings.
buses stop in the middle of the road,
their drivers abandoning them
to walk to empty cabins up north.
weeds begin to grow in the sidewalk cracks
with no thought for the overall
scheme of things.

this is not my home, my friend.

i live inside morning glories
and sunflowers,
blossoms thrown by the gods
to mortals
so that we might remember
what it was like

when we first arrived.

for mike bigger (1937-2011)

standing in this field
just outside red wing,
mike's sculpture
reminds me of su tung po.

massive
flaming red
steel i-beams
knot
and clang
and tower
up against
po's instructions:

"follow the advice of your common sense.
avoid the imperial audience chamber,
the eastern flowery hall."

the steel is thick and cold and bright
in the mid-winter sunlight,
even as stella races ahead
spurred on by the dream of rabbits and deer
and the absolute need to poop soon.
we have stopped here
at this midwestern sculpture park
to satisfy her needs.

my needs include a moment
with my old friend "big"
and his texas sized
constructions
(wasn't he from houston

or someplace like that?)

the snow is so white
against this second yellow sculpture.
he loved the poetry of size,
and the song that the wind makes
as it dreams of weight.

shit... mike, i miss you.

let's meet at the dubliner bar again,
that place on university and vandalia.
you could bad mouth the art world,
i would agree with you.
then, as we ordered our second beers,
i would mention su tung po again:

"wine is the best reward of merit."

softball

senior softball game.
the players move slow,
they are awkward.

sun's pelting them.
up to about 95 degrees today,
91% humidity, i swear.
the very definition of sin.
i thought this didn't happen in the desert.

nice breeze though,
where i sit here in the shade,
carpenters banging away
with their automatic nailers,
building an addition
on the house behind me.

when i was younger,
the buddha was my hero,
all that ascetic wandering,
the great, extreme path.
but he didn't have to deal
with walmart
and wave after wave
of shining yet stunningly ugly
automobiles.

the old guys playing ball
are way too serious about their game.
the batter's swing is bad
and the shortstop's throw
bounces on its way to first.

(the pavement melts
right in front of my eyes,
thereby sucking entire civilizations
down into the endless pit -
no one wants to live in a motel by the freeway,
everyone wants to live by the sea.)

a guy on the gray team
cracks a home run
over the left field fence.
is he 25 and just masquerading as a senior?

as a practicing psychic
it's hard to watch this political convention.
so much additional information,
so much duplicity.
i suppose if you live in the meat of things
it's much cleaner.
if trump is elected we will all disappear.
each of us will collapse
into a morass of rotting seaweed.

++++++++

i am the one
who keeps hope alive.

seagulls float within me.

I am that round stone
you found at point loma beach.

i pretend that everyone
understands what i say,

no matter
how many times
i say it.

take me with you

1.

just watched too much t.v.,
netflix on my computer,
a cop show.

trying to avoid my back hurting,
hurting day after day,
sometimes all day.
i'll take a hot shower and see if that helps.
maybe do a little tai chi,
some yoga.
do my physical therapy exercises.
say affirmations.

why do bodies hurt?
what greater purpose does pain serve?
i always tell young folks
that no one pays any attention
except thru suffering.
i am suffering.
what am i paying attention to?

it was supposed to hail tonight.
i was going to move my truck
to the drive-in car wash
to avoid it being damaged.
how could i have avoided being damaged?

2.

silence slides thru my body now.

it pools near the floor.
i type with my eyes closed,
then miss my youth for a minute or two,
down near the floor
where it lies
resting up against the cold.

3.

there is no such thing as suffering.
there is no such thing as the end of suffering.

4.

if i move too quickly
i will hit the window screens
over and over again
like all the wasps
racing from the october frosts
into my studio building.
if i move too slow,
i am nothing but the last
of the tourists,
left behind,
up to their asses
in snow.

5.

o great god of all things ancient, small, pathetic,

god of indigestion
and a heart that
continually skips beats,

take me with you
into the tall grass,
pull me down
and ask me to surrender
what is left
of my virgin soul.

dark studio

dark studio.
raining out, growing colder
here in western wisconsin
along the great river road.

film festival coming up soon,
i'll help out, meet folks
from new york and london,
drink local wine, pretend
we're the center of the cultural universe
for one night.

(threw the cards this morning.
the hanged man came up twice –
i use three decks mixed together -
looks like there is work to do,
inner stuff,
alchemical disciplines,
ritual needs...)

last week 40 vultures circled overhead,
i tried to count them all,
looping in lazy circles all across the sky,
flocking south,
dreaming of dead meat
alongside roads somewhere in arkansas,
rarely moving their wings,
singing in some old, strange song
i can't quite hear.

what if i followed them?
would it be better south of here?

note to lu

i started as a poet 53 years ago.
started as poet, stayed a poet.
sometimes a poet through my mouth,
sometimes through my hands,
sometimes through my ears or eyes.

words are a form of practical,
yet largely abstract mysticism.
i don't put words in my paintings.
or images. or color. or line.
i'm mostly gone when i make art.
i have no idea why what happens happens.
i could make something up, be an intellectual.
but i've grown bored with that.

no, its more like gardening:
plant seeds, water, fertilize, weed, harvest.
then plow it under
and hunker down through the winter.

except for me there is no winter,
winter is spring…
it all just keeps growing!

don't try and make too much sense
of words, lu.
if you do, you will become a linguist.
and then we will have to exile you
to far off places and have you de-liced.

let the words live on their own,
like the mayflies that hatch
and fly over the lake
and smash into the sides of our buildings,
all antennae and wings and eyes and feet.

sinking into the couch

sinking into the couch,
unable to sleep,
my coonhound snoring next to me,
the light grows
vaguely,
clumsily,
vacantly.

i am tired of a body that wakes me
in the middle of the night
with its continual
gentle,
solid,
pain.

i am tired of my hopes and dreams
being sponsored
by endless cycles
of noise
and pollution
and chatter.

i am tired of all the newspapers
and t.v.'s
and radios
and internet messages,
and the constant sagging toward
the darker,
dull
worlds.

the devil is loose again.

i know.
the chains were not quite tight,
the stake was not driven
deep enough into the ground.
now that bulbous
and dim man walks the world,
his breath stinking of champagne
and anorexic sycophants,
walks the world,
the damp, sour
smell of evil in tow,
wafting from him as he trails into the bushes
down below the power plant
where the backwaters of the river stink
and the brackish, green algae
scums away towards rot.

when i was younger, much younger,
i supposed that evil was a blind thing,
that it was merely the juxtaposition
of lack and ignorance.
i felt that all was curable,
that there were wings
hidden inside
each and every wound
scabbing over.

now i know better.
i've seen flowers wilt in seconds,
dog's legs curl into spirals like dead ferns.
i've heard the beast
move through the air
late at night
when dreams are sectioned
and bought off by fattened apparitions,

raised on the hog carcasses
of their mother's poisoned bellies.

when you meet the old one,
the leathered one,
the one with the foulness
rotting his breath -
when you face him,
if you can face him -

that moment
will sit inside you

screaming

for as long as there is a chance
that the sun can rise.

white out

snow blind on the ice,
can't see 15 feet
much less across the lake.

stella barks sharply at the snow
flying sideways
at our raw faces.

we turn and head back to shore
making our way
thru slabs of broken ice
and look up at the jetty bench,

bright cerulean blue

against a white,

white

sky.

on the miraculous nature of prayer

("the wound is the place
where the light enters you.")

richard is in st cloud prison.
i walk with a limp.
susan is working too hard.
i had to call the plumber
cause i fixed the plumbing.
i don't want it to rain today, but it will rain.
jurema is not available for consultation.
birds have nested in the air conditioner again.

"the wound is the place
where the light enters you."

soon i will sit on my meditation bench
and see if all and sundry flies and ticks
will leave the room.
i am hopeful that the lake
will not ice over this summer.

"the wound is the place
where the light enters you."

each morning gets shorter.
the best i can manage is baby yoga.
i am worried that the endlessly soaring vultures
have not come back.
the village has put in ugly blue l.e.d. lighting
to irritate us all into submission.
the café's workers scarf up
all the parking around my studio.

*"the wound is the place
where the light enters you."*

i am made of light.
there is no difference between light
and breath and love.
(no one understands this shit)
when i sit still and breathe,
i disappear into endlessness,
the breath, in and out,
in and out.
i relax into softness -
there is no dougie,
there is no not dougie.

*"the wound is the place
where the light enters you."*

richard comes out of prison early.
he has meditated the whole time
he was incarcerated
and no longer needs his meds.
my back feels great:
i am devoted to the old farts
yoga class i take in maiden rock.
susan works lovingly in her garden every day.
the plumber fixed everything in a half hour.
the rain turns my garden greener than green.
jurema can see me in st cloud in early june.

the sound of baby birds
sings out across the back yard.

"the wound is the place
where the light enters you."

— jalāl ad-dīn muhammad balkhī
(known as "rumi")

sitting in pho hoa

1.

sitting in pho hoa
i enjoy the spring rolls
and watch a 10 year old boy
throw snowballs into the air
and then smash them
with the arm of his coat.

o god the wonderful things to do
once the winter turns to spring,
the snow melting fast.

2.

yesterday, downriver,
i walked the jetty again with stella.
the light was bright then too,
so bright.

so bright i had to go back to the studio
to get my sunglasses,
my blue eyes hurting from the glare,
from the endlessness blue sky.

but the constant waves from the great lake
were sparkling diamonds,

sparkling diamonds.

and the ice grinding against the marina docks

was a thousand tiny birds chirping,

a thousand tiny birds chirping.

always

back to the weather,
always back to the weather.

but that's a good thing.
at least i am living outside more now,
parked in my studio building back yard
in a comfy padded patio chair,
october gray morning,
birds still singing, thank god…

my back doesn't hurt so much.
i am writing again,
poems,
memoirs,
letters.

the other night the door between worlds
dissolved a bit, souls crammed
up against the boundary,
aware that i could see them.
3 a.m. and i was both intrigued and a bit scared –
they were avaricious.
after a while i asked them to go away
and went back to sleep.

i am grateful for the lack of car noise
here in this small wisconsin river town.
i am grateful for so much room to make art,
for the vultures that turn and turn
in the skies overhead,
for the plodding dog walks
i take religiously twice a day,

walks that force me back out into the world
of dead fish grating away on the shoreline
and wasps grinding at my screen door.

soon, i will leave my feet
and travel upward.
it will be at dusk,
the very moment when the sun
reduces the horizon to brilliance.
i will leave my feet, my body, my prayers,
my thoughts of lasting,
and i will enter the new world,
the one that begins
where the night skies end,
that begins with
the absence of sounds,
with the absence of light.

an old man

from here by the shore
i hear the birds screaming.
not crows, grackles maybe.
i'm only beginning to be a bird guy.
tho it is true that crows
have talked to me since i was young.

the dead fish smell coming off the lake
is a bit strong,
so i move to a different bench
where there is more of a breeze.
the lake is quiet.
i am quiet.

in its own way everything melts.
seagulls crying melts into silver blue water
melts into the green bluffs on the far shore
melts into the voices of farmers
sitting in the café behind me.

      there never has been time.
      there never will be time.

      who am i is one endless myth,
      wave after wave after wave.

bugs crawling on my face.
i sneeze.
fisherman starts his boat motor.
an old man walks his dogs.

packing for the airport

harried and uptight,
i race to be ready to leave town
early tomorrow morning.

and suddenly susan mentions to me
that today is tuesday,
not wednesday...

and just as suddenly
the heavens open
and i feel a sense of grace
and expansiveness

as i fall, effortlessly, into time,

time created,

time gained,

time effortlessly given,

as if angels were in the room surrounding me
and lifting me with their wings.

trump wants a big military parade

1.

trump wants a big military parade
just like the french had.
only bigger,
much bigger.
a lot bigger and a lot better.
even bigger and better than the russians.

he's gonna need a special reviewing stand,
one where he can stand up really high,
front and center,
so he can review the troops
with all his generals,
and give them his papal blessings.
he needs one where all the cameras can see him.
from all the right angles,
where the world can watch this
the best military parade,
the biggest military parade,
like ever.

we're gonna need to do this up right.
we're gonna need to show
our respect for the troops.
money is no object here.
this is more important than all
those other things we are working on.
let's have an air force flyover while we're at it.
maybe we should get the navy to bring
some of its big boats into port for the day.
does washington have a port we can use?

and can we repaint all the tanks?
lets repaint them something prettier than camo,
camo is too ugly.
how about a brighter spring green,
something more perky?
or better yet gold,
i really like the color gold.

2.

in stockholm, wisconsin,
population 66,
the 4th of july parade
is very small.

folks wave small american flags,
the ones on little sticks.
kids ride their bikes in the parade.
there's a few folks on horses,
down from the farms up in the bluffs.
an occasional old tractor makes an appearance,
an orange allis chalmers
or a green and yellow john deere.
and more than one dog has been known
to walk the parade route
with or without their owner.
its over so quickly
that the floats and marchers
take a second run thru town,
which makes everyone
even happier.

there's not really any military involved.
though i'm sure they would be included

if they were stationed anywhere nearby.
but, the fire department up in lund rides
in their truck through town.
and the county sheriff shows up
and smiles a lot.

3.

its 8 pm.
the rabbits have come out with sunset.
they are chewing their way down to the lake.
farther up in the bluffs,
deer are starting to move slowly.
they too are grazing their way
towards water tonight.

lena's will have a few stragglers stay til 10.
the retired folks at stockholm park
will sit around campfires and talk
about where they will pull their trailers
this winter.

i head the 6 miles home,
grab a beer from the fridge,
and camp out in my hammock
in the back yard.
the crickets have taken up.
i can hear music from down on 1st,
probably from the breakwater bar
or maybe the dockside.
they're just close enough to hear,
far away enough to enjoy.

god I spent all those years sitting,
facing the wall as fiercely as I could,
trying to imitate zen masters,
trying to still my monkey mind.
it's taken me a long time in this life
to learn to let nothing happen,
well, nothing much.

a bit of breeze keeps the skeeters away.
the moon is rising over bob's place
across the street.
no sense getting up now
to go upstairs to bed.
i think i'll just
fall asleep

here.

**sitting in my pepin studio i read hafiz and fall
back in love... whereupon i read a facebook post
by historian timothy snyder on donald trump
and the rise of facism in the united states...**

1.

stella is fast asleep on the couch.
soon i will wake her and we will walk
on a gravel road in the woods
thru blue skies and marvelous
winter thaw air.

i will enjoy the sound of my feet on the gravel.
i will marvel at stella's sense of smell
as she stops every ten feet
to ecstatically devour every history
left for her by the animal world.

later i will build an installation
in my studio store front window,
a few dozen pink framed, pink paintings,
"thank you for marching"
written on the back of each,
hanging, hanging, hanging in the window
for townspeople to see
and wonder over.

or more likely they will spot them
and simply write it all off
as the ravings of that city artist guy,
crazy, liberal, privileged, rich...
an outsider, a tourist.

they won't see that millions marched
on november 21st, 2016, world-wide,
wearing pink hats and scarves,
holding high pink signs.
they won't see that the women took the reins,
took the battle took to the streets
in unprecedented numbers ...

2.

behind the president,
bannon, the henchman, is coughing.
he's been up all night, night after night,
planning the end of the republic.
the chessboard is in place,
he's 20 moves out,
he can see the whole game,
he's confident that this is his moment.
but his body is failing.
his skin is covered with rashes,
his eyes weep,
there are sores on the insides of his legs.
each time he lies to trump, to staff, to congress,
a boil on his side grows larger.
it is oozing slowly.
it smells of decay,
it smells of anger.

3.

eventually spring will come.
the ice will move out,
the lake will come alive with birds and fish.

the fishermen will come back,
the sailboats will revive,
the cafes will open,
humans will walk the street,
and musicians will serenade them.

but will we have eyes then?
will our bellies be intact?
or will someone have carved out our intestines
and spread them on racks by the water to dry
and be eaten next winter?
will someone have taken our shoes
and nailed them to the outside of the library,
an explicit note for all those that thought
that protest was the way.

i was not born to sit thru this.
i may be growing old, but i have put in my time,
i have teeth for wings.
i will not allow my grandchildren
to disappear before my eyes,
pulled out of school
and sent to far off camps
trained to be the next generation
of empty, mindless
flesh.

4.

may the unsated incubus
that sits in our highest office today
dissolve immediately
into a pool
of decaying flesh

beneath
his oval office desk.
and may those that surround him
and serve his dark consequence
join him on the floor,
their noisome liquids
disappearing
into cracks
in the aged oak parquet.
forever.

so be it.

wild game

in pepin
the sun is rising downriver,
orange and pink
with rays of gold,
rising over the sloughs
where the chippewa
meets the mississippi,
just west of nelson.

the lake is still solid ice,
three miles across
by twenty-three miles long.
there are still ice fishing houses
in small villages
fifty yards out from the pepin marina,
in the middle of the river near maiden rock,
and on the frontenac side of lake city.

i've never really understood
sitting in the raw cold
in a pop-up tent on a folding stool
staring at a hole in the ice
waiting for a small fish
to find my hook.

i'm more of a tracker-hunter myself.
though wild game
in the art world
is rare.

the antelope wife

the brain goes into overload.
i am doing this to myself.

put my new collage up on instagram:
 "massive confusion in the states
over ascension of comrade trump
to the heavenly throne
(resist evil embody light)".

franzen and sharra frank and josh
have already liked it.
somebody named jeff.squazoart likes it.
evantramblane, student painter
somewhere likes it.
then the photo slides over to facebook
(how'd i do that?).
hannah found it. richard knopf.
even rueben urrutia
(is he here or in mexico?).
back on instagram,
sarafrederica likes my art.
she shoots architecture in b&w,
in italy somewhere,
looks like torino.
i think i'll follow her.

++++++++

this morning the sun rose steel hard,
a bronze yellow knot splaying out
over the river,
frozen bank to bank,

frozen exactly cold,
frozen forever.

i was reading in bed again,
the antelope wife.
i'm on some kinda louise erdrich kick,
seven of her novels now,
six in the last five months.

i read from 6 a.m. to 8,
crawled out of bed into the cold room,
once a masonic lodge,
turned up the heat,
made oatmeal with yoghurt and flax,
raisins, walnuts, apples,

then went down 23 stairs to the studio,
turned the heat up there too,
opened the drapes and let my plants breathe.
then, on down into the basement
to check on a project,
i start to clean up for work.
this will be a good day.

+++++++

i'm wondering what it's like
to sit in the belly of an antelope.
to feel its flesh as it rebounds
across the prairie.
i am looking from its eyes.
i can see forever.
understanding is not the key,
i don't make plans,
i graze on what little the prairie affords.

my dad shot an antelope
in wyoming in the fifties.
he musta been hunting with his cousins.
i gave a photo of him with that pronghorn
to my son, dad a refugee from the depression
way back in the '30's,
graduated from greybull high school.
not enough to eat with his folks back in iowa.

i gave my son that antelope mount for his cabin.
the hair was falling out, it's been 60 years.
i wish my father was here,
we could see that hunt together.
he could describe it from his hunter's eyes,
the binoculars searching,
the slow inevitable walk from the truck
with his rifle,
the crawl to the edge of the rise,
the surprise that the male is so close.

i would look back from my spot on the horizon,
then, moving quickly, bounding,
my rump muscles tight,
my black antlers sharp in the sunlight,
the smell of fear in my black nose,
quivering, quivering,
the sweat just above my black eyes.
something between wonder
and darkness
ringing in the air,

something desperate.

gift

i have so many stories to write,
i'm not sure i will write any of them.
its so easy to take out a dvd
and watch someone destroy a planet
or a love affair or a couplet.
its so hard to remember what happened,
what is happening...

painting is easier,
just move into the larger world,
the world unleashed and unguided
and untouched
except for a bit of ochre here and there,
a bit of brilliant yellow or pike's green.

i just put in the time,
all the while letting the monkey between my ears
gather nuts in the forest,
listen to bach descending, ascending,
listen to sports radio rambling forever,
or the news, the endless driveling news...

but my hands work,
they have a gift of their own
i don't really know them well,
i try and stay out of their way.

and they plow on, they just plow on,

morning to night,
day after day
after day.

the rain came down

the rain came down in sheets
in swirls
in cones
in walls
in nightmares

it came down from the north
from the south
it came from the right
from the left
it flew sideways at all the buildings in town
it rose up from the earth in wave after wave

the rain lied
it cried
it debated national policy
it spoke in hushed tones on the corners
it wailed in its bed like a baby

it dumped
and planted itself everywhere
and then it ran home
with its tail between its legs

the rain spied
it challenged
it broadcast itself
it advertised in the shopper
it made mincemeat of gardens

the rain came with thunder
with lightning

it came alone
in came in hordes
it came from both the east and west
simultaneously

i sat it out on the second floor
i closed every window and shade and drape
i closed every door and holed up in my bedroom
i refused to go to the refrigerator
i refused to go to the bathroom
and brush my teeth
i lay in the bed in the dark
and still the storm got in

the rain pounded at the roof
it pounded on the walls
it sought me out where i was hiding
and asked me questions that weren't
in the preparatory materials
we received in the mail

the lightening flickered
on and off
on and off
like a disturbed child abandoned
in the front seat of the car
endlessly playing with the headlights

the thunder was endless, distant, rolling,
magnificent, lonely
it hammered me
it smashed me
it annihilated all thoughts i had of peace
it was the uncle that just couldn't quit drinking

but all things change
eventually
the rain slowed
it mellowed
it lightened
it sang in sugary minor keys

the grass grew stronger
it raised itself green to the skies in gratitude
it whispered about sun
maybe the next morning
was the news i was hearing around the block

and sure enough the sun rose the next day
and there was singing everywhere
the big lake was singing,
sending waves in all directions
the village residents were singing
by shopping at paul and fran's
i started singing too
i was in charge of the color
of the sky that morning
i chose blue
a deep baby blue
that i applied in layers
when i was on my lunch break.

yes, i chose the blue
that is the voice light makes
when its had a good long rest
and a nice breakfast
with the wife.

4 songs for my father

(for donald gabino padilla)

1.

walking thru this bed of roses
i think about the lions you use to bend
into shapes and sounds and smells
until all the businesses in the western world
fell under your spell
and honored you
in their dreams.

2.

this time i bend low
and start to pray the prayer of small things ...
of rocks and paper and even beer cans:
i want this home of mine
to be your home again.
i want the birds that sit on the water
to talk about you
and sing until you materialize
like the fish that wait on the river bottom
until it's time to fly thru the air
for that one sweet
dark moment.

3.

father, if you were alive now,
would i still feel so heavy?

4.

in the beginning of this last summer
i saw a vision of the land
i will buy some day
on a hilltop
down along the eastern side
of the mississippi
a couple of hours from here.

there'll be a grove of trees there,
downhill from the barn
that susan and i make
into my studio get-away.
and hannah and eli's kids
will join us there for long hot summer days.
i'll take them down to the river
in the middle of the day to bathe
and splash around.
then, just as it gets dark, we'll walk
to the top of the hill,
to the place where we can see best,
where we can see miles in every direction.
that's where you'll lay beside us
as we watch the horizon turn
from orange to dark blue,
as we wish our wishes upon shooting stars
and smell the sweet, sweet grasses
turn our day into night.

northeast minneapolis, 1997

acknowledgements

i would like to recognize my editor, the late ron chastain, for his sweetness, his brains, his encouragement. i would also like to thank karen wilcox for her organizing instincts and persistence. and thanks to ted king, king of performance poetics and true wit. my gratitude to xavier tavera for our long running and deeply creative friendship. i would also like to acknowledge all my teachers: the list is long, too long for here... but i am grateful.

and, o god, i can't leave out hannah and eli, and paco and birdie. thank you for your love. but most especially, i would like to thank susan jacobsen, limitless in her devotion, endless in her support, a blessing in her patience and intelligence.

also, i would like to recognize writers: poet robert bly for his friendship and all those wisening retreats in the north woods; the beats, especially, gary snyder, whose books galvanized my hitch-hiking kerouac style all over 60's north america; gabriel garcia marquez and louise erdrich – the two of whom seduced me back into a love of storytelling; and, finally, frederico garcia lorca, for his absolute understanding of the beauty of words:

 " ...mil violines caben en la palma mi mano."

(" ...a thousand violins fit in the palm of my hand.")

dougie padilla

long ago and far away i was a young poet. i wrote
constantly. then came the viet nam war and all the
protests. and then came san francisco and psychedelics
and communes around the country. a psychotic break
came. heart failure came. and ashrams and organic
farming with horses. eventually, there were kids and
houses and marriage and businesses. and even grand
kids...

now it's fifty years later and out of the blue poetry
returned quick and sure. i'd moved my art studio to
rural wisconsin to beat rising rents in the city, to
concentrate on my painting, to meditate, be in nature, to
face my aloneness. once there, i started working on my
memoirs. instead, poems begin pouring out. in a year
and a half there were sixty or so sitting in a notebook
finished and ready to be born into the world. it was a
miracle.

www.dougiepadilla.com